Francis Frith's
DOWN THE THAMES

PHOTOGRAPHIC MEMORIES

Francis Frith's
DOWN THE THAMES

◆

Martin Andrew

First published in the United Kingdom in 2000 by
Frith Book Company Ltd

Hardback Edition 2000
ISBN 1-85937-121-3

Paperback Edition 2001
ISBN 1-85937-278-3

Hardback Reprinted in 2001

British Library Cataloguing in Publication Data

Francis Frith's Down the Thames
Martin Andrew

Frith Book Company Ltd
Frith's Barn, Teffont,
Salisbury, Wiltshire SP3 5QP
Tel: +44 (0) 1722 716 376
Email: info@frithbook.co.uk
www.frithbook.co.uk

Printed and bound in Great Britain

AS WITH ANY HISTORICAL DATABASE THE FRITH ARCHIVE IS CONSTANTLY BEING CORRECTED AND IMPROVED
AND THE PUBLISHERS WOULD WELCOME INFORMATION ON OMISSIONS OR INACCURACIES

CONTENTS

FRANCIS FRITH: *Victorian Pioneer*

FRANCIS FRITH, Victorian founder of the world-famous photographic archive, was a complex and multitudinous man. A devout Quaker and a highly successful Victorian businessman, he was both philosophic by nature and pioneering in outlook.

By 1855 Francis Frith had already established a wholesale grocery business in Liverpool, and sold it for the astonishing sum of £200,000, which is the equivalent today of over £15,000,000. Now a multi-millionaire, he was able to indulge his passion for travel. As a child he had pored over travel books written by early explorers, and his fancy and imagination had been stirred by family holidays to the sublime mountain regions of Wales and Scotland. 'What a land of spirit-stirring and enriching scenes and places!' he had written. He was to return to these scenes of grandeur in later years to 'recapture the thousands of vivid and tender memories', but with a different purpose. Now in his thirties, and captivated by the new science of photography, Frith set out on a series of pioneering journeys to the Nile regions that occupied him from 1856 until 1860.

INTRIGUE AND ADVENTURE

He took with him on his travels a specially-designed wicker carriage that acted as both dark-room and sleeping chamber. These far-flung journeys were packed with intrigue and adventure. In his life story, written when he was sixty-three, Frith tells of being held captive by bandits, and of fighting 'an awful midnight battle to the very point of surrender with a deadly pack of hungry, wild dogs'. Sporting flowing Arab costume, Frith arrived at Akaba by camel seventy years before Lawrence, where he encountered 'desert princes and rival sheikhs, blazing with jewel-hilted swords'.

During these extraordinary adventures he was assiduously exploring the desert regions bordering the Nile and patiently recording the antiquities and peoples with his camera. He was the first photographer to venture beyond the sixth cataract. Africa was still the mysterious 'Dark Continent', and Stanley and Livingstone's historic meeting was a decade into the future. The conditions for picture taking confound belief. He laboured for hours in his wicker dark-room in the sweltering heat of the desert, while the volatile chemicals fizzed dangerously in their trays. Often he was forced to work in remote tombs and caves where conditions were cooler. Back in London he exhibited his photographs and was 'rapturously cheered' by members of the Royal Society. His reputation as a photographer was made overnight. An eminent modern historian has likened their impact on the population of the time to that on our own generation of the first photographs taken on the surface of the moon.

VENTURE OF A LIFE-TIME

Characteristically, Frith quickly spotted the opportunity to create a new business as a specialist publisher of photographs. He lived in an era of immense and sometimes violent change. For the poor in the early part of Victoria's reign work was a drudge and the hours long, and people had precious little free time to enjoy themselves.

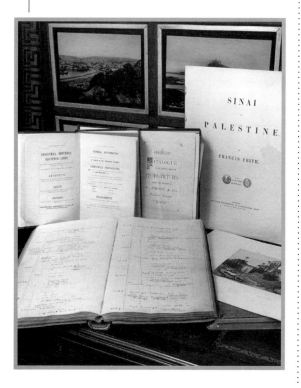

Most had no transport other than a cart or gig at their disposal, and had not travelled far beyond the boundaries of their own town or village. However, by the 1870s, the railways had threaded their way across the country, and Bank Holidays and half-day Saturdays had been made obligatory by Act of Parliament. All of a sudden the ordinary working man and his family were able to enjoy days out and see a little more of the world.

With characteristic business acumen, Francis Frith foresaw that these new tourists would enjoy having souvenirs to commemorate their days out. In 1860 he married Mary Ann Rosling and set out with the intention of photographing every city, town and village in Britain. For the next thirty years he travelled the country by train and by pony and trap, producing fine photographs of seaside resorts and beauty spots that were keenly bought by millions of Victorians. These prints were painstakingly pasted into family albums and pored over during the dark nights of winter, rekindling precious memories of summer excursions.

THE RISE OF FRITH & CO

Frith's studio was soon supplying retail shops all over the country. To meet the demand he gathered about him a small team of photographers, and published the work of independent artist-photographers of the calibre of Roger Fenton and Francis Bedford. In order to gain some understanding of the scale of Frith's business one only has to look at the catalogue issued by Frith & Co in 1886: it runs to some 670

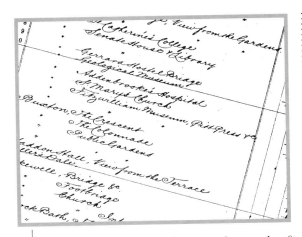

pages, listing not only many thousands of views of the British Isles but also many photographs of most European countries, and China, Japan, the USA and Canada – note the sample page shown above from the hand-written *Frith & Co* ledgers detailing pictures taken. By 1890 Frith had created the greatest specialist photographic publishing company in the world, with over 2,000 outlets – more than the combined number that Boots and WH Smith have today! The picture on the right shows the *Frith & Co* display board at Ingleton in the Yorkshire Dales. Beautifully constructed with mahogany frame and gilt inserts, it could display up to a dozen local scenes.

POSTCARD BONANZA

The ever-popular holiday postcard we know today took many years to develop. In 1870 the Post Office issued the first plain cards, with a pre-printed stamp on one face. In 1894 they allowed other publishers' cards to be sent through the mail with an attached adhesive halfpenny stamp. Demand grew rapidly, and in 1895 a new size of postcard was permitted called the

court card, but there was little room for illustration. In 1899, a year after Frith's death, a new card measuring 5.5 x 3.5 inches became the standard format, but it was not until 1902 that the divided back came into being, with address and message on one face and a full-size illustration on the other. *Frith & Co* were in the vanguard of postcard development, and Frith's sons Eustace and Cyril continued their father's monumental task, expanding the number of views offered to the public and recording more and more places in Britain, as the coasts and countryside were opened up to mass travel.

Francis Frith died in 1898 at his villa in Cannes, his great project still growing. The archive he created continued in business for another seventy years. By 1970 it contained over a third of a million pictures of 7,000 cities, towns and villages. The massive photographic record Frith has left to us stands as a living monument to a special and very remarkable man.

Frith's Archive: *A Unique Legacy*

FRANCIS FRITH'S legacy to us today is of immense significance and value, for the magnificent archive of evocative photographs he created provides a unique record of change in 7,000 cities, towns and villages throughout Britain over a century and more. Frith and his fellow studio photographers revisited locations many times down the years to update their views, compiling for us an enthralling and colourful pageant of British life and character.

We tend to think of Frith's sepia views of Britain as nostalgic, for most of us use them to conjure up memories of places in our own lives with which we have family associations. It often makes us forget that to Francis Frith they were records of daily life as it was actually being lived in the cities, towns and villages of his day. The Victorian age was one of great and often bewildering change for ordinary people, and though the pictures evoke an impression of slower times, life was as busy and hectic as it is today.

We are fortunate that Frith was a photographer of the people, dedicated to recording the minutiae of everyday life. For it is this sheer wealth of visual data, the painstaking chronicle of changes in dress, transport, street layouts, buildings, housing, engineering and landscape that captivates us so much today. His remarkable images offer us a powerful link with the past and with the lives of our ancestors.

TODAY'S TECHNOLOGY

Computers have now made it possible for Frith's many thousands of images to be accessed almost instantly. In the Frith archive today, each photograph is carefully 'digitised' then stored on a CD Rom. Frith archivists can locate a single photograph amongst thousands within seconds. Views can be catalogued and sorted under a variety of categories of place and content to the immediate benefit of researchers. Inexpensive reference prints can be created for them at the touch of a mouse button, and a wide range of books and other printed materials assembled and published for a wider, more general readership - in the next twelve months over a hundred Frith local history titles will be published! The

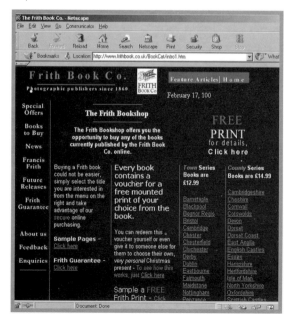

See Frith at www. frithbook.co.uk

day-to-day workings of the archive are very different from how they were in Francis Frith's time: imagine the herculean task of sorting through eleven tons of glass negatives as Frith had to do to locate a particular sequence of pictures! Yet the archive still prides itself on maintaining the same high standards of excellence laid down by Francis Frith, including the painstaking cataloguing and indexing of every view.

It is curious to reflect on how the internet now allows researchers in America and elsewhere greater instant access to the archive than Frith himself ever enjoyed. Many thousands of individual views can be called up on screen within seconds on one of the Frith internet sites, enabling people living continents away to revisit the streets of their ancestral home town, or view places in Britain where they have enjoyed holidays. Many overseas researchers welcome the chance to view special theme selections, such as transport, sports, costume and ancient monuments.

We are certain that Francis Frith would have heartily approved of these modern developments, for he himself was always working at the very limits of Victorian photographic technology.

THE VALUE OF THE ARCHIVE TODAY

Because of the benefits brought by the computer, Frith's images are increasingly studied by social historians, by researchers into genealogy and ancestory, by architects, town planners, and by teachers and schoolchildren involved in local history projects. In addition, the archive offers every one of us a unique opportunity to examine the places where we and our families have lived and worked down the years. Immensely successful in Frith's own era, the archive is now, a century and more on, entering a new phase of popularity.

THE PAST IN TUNE WITH THE FUTURE

Historians consider the Francis Frith Collection to be of prime national importance. It is the only archive of its kind remaining in private ownership and has been valued at a million pounds. However, this figure is now rapidly increasing as digital technology enables more and more people around the world to enjoy its benefits.

Francis Frith's archive is now housed in an historic timber barn in the beautiful village of Teffont in Wiltshire. Its founder would not recognize the archive office as it is today. In place of the many thousands of dusty boxes containing glass plate negatives and an all-pervading odour of photographic chemicals, there are now ranks of computer screens. He would be amazed to watch his images travelling round the world at unimaginable speeds through network and internet lines.

The archive's future is both bright and exciting. Francis Frith, with his unshakeable belief in making photographs available to the greatest number of people, would undoubtedly approve of what is being done today with his lifetime's work. His photographs, depicting our shared past, are now bringing pleasure and enlightenment to millions around the world a century and more after his death.

DOWN THE THAMES – *An Introduction*

'Sweet Thames, run softly....' Edmund Spenser

THIS BOOK TAKES the form of an imaginary journey down the River Thames from near its source a few miles south of Cirencester in Gloucestershire down through Oxford, Reading and London into the mud-flat lands of the wide Thames Estuary as far as Shoeburyness, or Sheerness, where it in effect debouches into the North Sea. This is a total journey of about 215 miles, making the Thames the longest river wholly in England. We shall see it change from a stream through a rural village, powering the occasional water-mill, to a mighty trade highway teeming with towed barges and navigated via pound locks, which by-pass the treacherous weirs, into the calmer waters that flow through the great city of London and onwards to the sea.

What is seen on the banks and near the river has changed greatly in some places, and remarkably little in others; this book spans about three quarters of a century in its head-long progress through time and space. Old Father Thames just keeps on flowing ... It has seen the mighty London docks rise to become the busiest and wealthiest in human history, a vast entrepot for the world's goods and products flowing through a great industrial city. These vast docks, excavated on the north and south banks, and lined by cranes, derricks and railways besides millions of square feet of warehouses, flourished from 1799 until finally closing in 1981. Their trade moved further east to the container port of Tilbury. To some extent, we are all blinded by the Industrial Revolution in the North of England to the vast amount of manufacturing and processing that took place in London. Indeed, until about 1800 there were more steam engines in London than in Lancashire, and until the mid 19th century London's manufacturing output was unmatched anywhere in England, let alone the world. Since that time the emphasis has gradually shifted elsewhere; now London's polluting industries have largely been transformed into service industries and offices, always a major element. The docks are now Dockland, a vast complex of offices, houses and flats interspersed with the water of some of the retained docks, which have become ornamental lakes and marinas for the inhabitants. The major benefit for the Thames is the greater cleanliness of the water: it was once described as 110% effluent as it passed the Houses of Parliament in the 1840s, assisting King Cholera and King Typhoid in their deadly work. Salmon have now returned since their disappearance late in the 18th century.

The river's primary function, even down past the Pool of London, is pleasure. Boating became immensely popular with all social classes in the later 19th century. No view of the river on a Sunday was complete without a scrum of skiffs, punts, sailing boats, canoes, steam launches and all kinds of pleasure craft jostling for the water and converging to cram the locks that by-passed the all-too-frequent weirs. All this is superbly described in that comic masterpiece by Jerome K Jerome, 'Three Men in a Boat', published in 1889; it gives a splendid picture of messing about in boats between Kingston and Oxford. Arrayed in their bright striped blazers and straw boaters, flannels, deck shoes, ladies' white dresses and parasols, the new mobile middle and lower middle classes, now with more leisure and disposable income, began the transformation of the river from trade artery to leisure facility. This new role was necessitated by the railway age, which supplanted canals and rivers as the main means of shipping goods.

It was as well that Jerome and his friends took to the water, for without them, and the need for flood control, water conservation and processing the river would not have been maintained as it has: witness the dereliction of many canals, until leisure use and enthusiasts stimulated their gradual restoration in recent years. The main areas having trade as a main

element now lie east of London, with the main container port to the west of Tilbury on the Essex bank, out in the estuarine Thames.

In this book there are two main themes beloved of the Frith photographers: the Thames crossings - that is, bridges - and the locks and weirs. The latter cope with its total descent of 250 feet from the first lock, St

were a normal feature of most weirs until well into the 19th century, and the censuses of 1841, 1861 and 1881 list fishermen among the working-class populations of towns such as Henley and Marlow. Other river-dependent occupations included brewers, brewery workers, mill workers, bargees and wharfingers. Many industries took their power source from

John's Lock at Lechlade, to the last, Richmond Lock and Half-Tide Weir, involving a total of 45 locks. Below Richmond the river is little above sea level and wholly tidal, although Teddington above Richmond is generally regarded as the limit of the tidal Thames - a fact allegedly known by every schoolboy, at least in my young day in the 1950s.

The river had been a trade route of supreme importance from early times, and navigational problems and weirs were constant causes of friction with fishermen and riparian owners. Those earlier fishermen were not leisure anglers, but people dependent on fish for their livelihood. Eel traps

the river by means of water-wheels, and many of the mill buildings survive, although not normally as mills but as offices, flats and other uses. The river's waterwheels provided the power for flour, paper and gunpowder making, leather and tanning, and any industrial process needing power or large amounts of water. Even now, huge quantities of Thames water are extracted, and usually partly returned to the river, from the millions of gallons a day diverted into Didcot Power Station to much lesser quantities for processing plants along the river. Some mills remain as important riverside buildings, providing valuable links with the past, such as Hambleden Mill, now flats, Mapledurham Mill, or

Cricklade Mill, now a house, while others have vanished utterly, including those in Marlow and Reading or Shiplake.

The current locks, which range from the modest ones on the upper Thames to the giant at Teddington (650 feet long and capable of handling eight barges and their tug in one go), emerged during the late 18th century. These are the 'pound locks': the boats are empounded while the water level is equalised to that of the way the boats wish to go by means of sluices, which fill or empty the lock as required.

For many hundreds of years the predecessor of the pound lock was the 'flash' lock, which had only one pair of gates. It is hair-raising to describe how they worked downstream. The gates would be opened in or beside a weir, and the river water thundered through, sweeping or 'flashing' the barge or boat through. The gates would then be closed, usually by means of a series of 'paddles', rectangular sluice planks attached to long poles, and the river would return to its previous level until a further boat or barge arrived and the perilous process would begin again. If a boat wished to come upstream, the paddles would be removed and the boat would be hauled through the gap in the weir by men hauling on stout ropes or by means of a heavy capstan winch. The last surviving capstan, on the north bank below Wittington, west of Marlow, has recently been restored to working condition by Wycombe District Council. The process was a hazardous one; over the years many bargees were drowned when boats were capsized or foundered.

The pound lock was a major advance, not only in safety. It was also more welcome to fishermen and water mill owners, for a busy

day through the flash locks could seriously lower the overall river level to reduce waterwheel efficiency, particularly in summer when water levels are particularly low; also, all the fish could be washed downstream. Pound locks replaced flash locks in a remarkably gradual programme. Many were changed from 1771 to about 1810, but ownership problems left many in place. It took the Thames Navigation Act of 1866 to give greater powers to the Thames Commissioners to secure the removal of the last few flash locks in the midst of weirs - these rendered water management a nightmare until the 1930s, despite the locks nearby. The pound locks themselves have mostly been rebuilt several times, and currently a massive programme of lock and weir reconstruction is just coming to an end. This is not surprising: river scour, the enormous power of water, and the frequent use of the gates and machinery necessitate frequent repair and overhaul, particularly as the first locks mostly had turf side walls.

The Thames was indeed a major trade route, with vast tonnages of goods and raw materials being laboriously hauled by ropes up and down stream by gangs of men until the 19th century, when horses put the bargees out of work; goods also travelled by sail and oar in favourable conditions. Sailing barges, once a familiar sight on the lower Thames and in the Estuary, are now transmogrified into leisure craft, and are the preserve of restorers, rather than hauliers. A remarkable view of late 17th-century barges on the river can be seen in oil paintings of the river in Henley and its environs by the Dutch artist Jan Siberechts. Grain, malt, bricks, wool, cloth, coal, flints, limestone, timber and a hundred other products and raw materials made their way up and down the Thames and its tributaries. Canals, such as the Kennet and Avon, opened in 1810, and the Thames and Severn, opened in 1789, all helped maintain the river's supremacy in supplying and trading with London.

To jump a couple of centuries, the leisure boom was captured in a famous painting of Boulters Lock, near Maidenhead, by Edward Gregory, first exhibited in 1897. The pressure on lock mechanisms became enormous, with hundreds of boats passing each way on a Saturday afternoon and a Sunday. To reduce the problem, and speed small craft on their way, boat elevators, ramps with rollers, were installed at some of the busiest locks to reduce congestion. Those at Boulters, Teddington and Richmond Locks are shown in this book, as well as a very narrow lock at Teddington, the Skiff Lock, another leisure adjustment on the river system.

The river as far as Staines had been granted to the City of London by Richard the Lion Heart in 1197, but coherent management of the whole river only started in the 18th century with the appointment of Thames Navigational Commissioners in a 1751 act of parliament. Proving somewhat ineffectual, the Thames Act of 1770 laid the foundations for modern management of the whole river; it resulted in the replacement of many of the flash locks by pound locks, a technical device borrowed from canal design. However, things were still not ideal, particularly as in the earlier 19th century traffic increased vastly with leisure boating and with the advent of steam power for both commerce and passenger carrying. The commissioners were responsible not only for the locks, weirs and the state of the river banks, but also for the towing paths alongside.

In 1857 the Thames Conservancy was

formed; their coat of arms, and that of the City of London, can be seen on the date plaques of many lock-keeper's cottages. The Port of London Authority was set up in 1908 to be responsible for the port of London and all aspects of the river in and to the east of London.

And all the time the Thames passes beneath many bridges of outstanding quality, from the massive ironwork of Hammersmith Bridge, the elegance of Marlow's suspension bridge, or the glorious stonework of Richmond Bridge (1770s), Staines Bridge (1830) or Maidenhead Bridge (1770s) - and, of course, that symbol of London, Tower Bridge. There are also less wonderful bridges, such as the woeful Walton on Thames Bridge (1860s). This book also includes some of the best 'lost' bridges, Waterloo (1810s) and London (1820s) - not that their replacements are unsuccessful. Certainly the bridges across the river have fascinating histories, including the smaller ones such as Lechlade's Ha'penny toll bridge (1790s) or the Whitchurch toll bridge (late 19th century).

This book has its photographs divided into five chapters. The first starts below Thames Head and follows it down as far as Wallingford via Lechlade and Oxford, where, it seems, an 18th-century affectation with no historical basis termed the Thames above Dorchester 'the Isis'. Chapter two follows the river from Streatley through the Goring Gap to pass Reading and Henley to Marlow: real 'Three Men in a Boat' territory. Chapter three takes us as far as Richmond and the last of the river's weirs and locks, while the fourth chapter leads us into the metropolis to finish at Tower Bridge. The last chapter heads into the Thames Estuary past the wonderful Thames

Barrier at Woolwich, built to defend the city from flood surges from the North Sea, and passes below the Queen Elizabeth Bridge to head for where the Estuary merges with the North Sea near Shoeburyness. It is a mighty river, passing through wonderful countryside in Oxfordshire, Gloucestershire, Buckinghamshire and Berkshire, ranging from the meadows around Lechlade to the tree-clad river cliffs below Cliveden. Then there are the towns and villages near to or on the river, the mellow golden Cotswold limestones of Lechlade or Ashton Keynes, the stone-built colleges of Oxford, the splendid towns of Henley and Marlow, the shattered husks of Maidenhead and Staines, and then one of the greatest cities in the world: London.

This introduction, I hope, conveys the fascination and excitement of this great river; I hope, too, that the selection of photographs goes some way to capturing the character of the river in its various moods and the very different landscapes through which it flows, now cleaner than it has been for a couple of hundred years. As a parting shot I commend you to read or re-read Jerome K Jerome's 'Three Men in a Boat', an affectionate and amusing snapshot of the river in 1889, close to the date of most of the oldest views in the book and highly evocative. My own memories from part of my boyhood in Ealing in the 1950s Include the irridescent flash of a kingfisher in a muddy Brentford creek and trains of lumbering barges hauled by dirty ancient tugs along a brown and unappetising looking river. All that has changed: the barges have gone, and coxed fours and pleasure boats now ply along a clean and healthy river.

ASHTON KEYNES, CHURCH WALK WITH MILL HOUSE AND THE RIVER THAMES c1955 A144305

Our photographic tour starts some four or five miles from the traditional source of the Thames in this delightful Cotswold stone village, through which the young river flows as little more than a vigorous stream. It formerly powered a watermill with the Mill House on the right and its mill-leet to its left.

ASHTON KEYNES, HIGH ROAD c1955 A144301

This Wiltshire village is known locally as the village of four crosses, all medieval. This view looks along High Road with Church Walk on the left past the cross shaft, and the young Thames just out of picture on the left. Cocks House, in the distance at the junction with Back Street, is unchanged.

CRICKLADE
St Mary's Church c1955

Cricklade, ten miles from the Thames source, is an ancient town with evidence of Anglo-Saxon town walls as well as of Roman occupation. It has two medieval churches, the splendidly towered St Sampson behind the High Street, and the less grand St Mary's at the north end of the High Street, which has this fine complete 14th-century churchyard cross.

◆

CRICKLADE
High Street c1955

This small Wiltshire market town has a long, roughly north-south High Street, seen here looking north from the junction with Bath Road. The houses on the right were demolished to improve the junction with Calcutt Road, but little else has changed. The 1897 Diamond Jubilee clock tower survives outside The Vale pub.

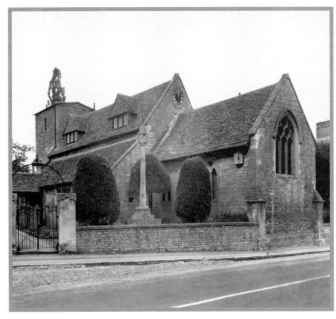

CRICKLADE, ST MARY'S CHURCH c1955 C300002

CRICKLADE, HIGH STREET c1955 C300003

INGLESHAM, LITTLE HOLME YHA c1955 I26001

Moving downstream, it is no use the hopeful walker knocking on the door of this early 19th-century farmhouse, Littleholme, in Upper Inglesham, hoping for a bed: it is no longer, as it was in the 1950s, a Youth Hostel. Next to it, however, is the Inglesham Forge Restaurant, so at least the walker could eat.

LECHLADE, THE RIVER c1955 L147045

About twenty-five miles downstream from its source we reach the stone-built town of Lechlade on the Gloucestershire bank of the Thames. The Ha'penny Bridge was built in 1792 to replace a ferry. It is an elegant single arch with a tall, pyramid-roofed tollhouse, and so named because of the original crossing toll.

LECHLADE, THE CHURCH FROM THE RIVER C1955 L147057
Looking north from roughly the same viewpoint on the south bank of the Thames, the Perpendicular Gothic parish church with its tall spire, one of Gloucestershire's fine 'wool' churches, dominates the view. The willows have gone or been replaced, and there is more building in the plots behind the High Street on the left, but the scene is still just as tranquil.

LECHLADE, RIVERSIDE TEA GARDENS c1955 L147049

The warehouse on the right is now the Riverside Free House, but it and the dock reflect the commerce that made Lechlade a prosperous medieval town, where wool and cheese were loaded onto barges for shipment down river. Nowadays the fields to the far left are a leisure yacht park - yachts are the river's modern traffic - and the tea garden in the middle distance has long gone.

LECHLADE, THE SQUARE c1955 L147041

The focus of the town is the triangular medieval market place, with the best buildings on its south side: the Old Vicarage of 1805 with its Venetian ground floor windows, mansard roof and battlemented porch, Maple House beyond with its battlemented parapet and, of course, the superb St Lawrence's parish church's tower and spire.

LECHLADE, THE SQUARE C1955 L147063

This view looks north out of the Market Place, past the corner of St John Street, with the Old Vicarage on the right. This is Burford Street, with stone houses of all shapes and sizes from cottages to the Swan Hotel on the left, a part-Tudor building, and the urbane Georgian of Ryton House on the right with its four brick chimneystacks.

LECHLADE, THE MILL AND WATERFALL C1955 L147037

Lechlade Mill, a mile east of the town, was powered by the River Leach which reached the Thames just below St John's Lock. The mill buildings on the left are now converted into a house with further extensions, but well designed, and in a very pretty location.

OXFORD, THE EIGHTS 1922 72063
The Thames, or Isis, plays an important role in
Oxford University life. Here, seen from the tow path
along the west bank, looking north towards
Christchurch Meadow, the annual Eights Week is in
full swing at the end of May when the college boats
race each other. Spectators in up-to-the-minute 1922
fashions look on from the shore and from punts.

OXFORD, THE EIGHTS 1906 53695

This view, taken from Folly Bridge at the south end of St Aldate's Street, is of an earlier Eights Week with the Christchurch Meadow bank lined with the College Barges. Each college had its own ornate barge: you can see one moored at the Swan Hotel in Streatley further downstream.

OXFORD, ON THE RIVER 1922 72053

It is still Eights Week, but this time in 1922 and during a lull in the racing; this view is taken from just beyond where the River Cherwell meets the Thames. The water seethes with punts, and one of the college barges is in the distance. Many of the latter had a balustraded upper deck and a large flagpole for the college colours.

OXFORD, VIEW ON THE CHERWELL 1906 53704
Punting is and was a very popular pastime, and anyone, not only students, can hire a punt. The River Cherwell is quieter than the Thames; a popular run on a summer evening is up for a drink to the Victoria and Albert pub at Old Marston, whose garden runs down to the river.

OXFORD, FROM MAGDALEN TOWER 1890 26802

From the vantage point of Magdalen College belfry we look westwards along the High Street towards some of the wondrous 'dreaming spires', including the 14th-century spire of St Mary's Church; to its right is the dome of the sublime Radcliffe Camera, built in the 1740s by James Gibbs. To the left is Jackson's splendid Jacobethan Examination Schools, completed only eight years before this view was taken.

OXFORD, HIGH STREET 1922 71992

This view looks past Queen's College with its early 18th-century Baroque frontage to the High, the pedimented wings framing a gatehouse surmounted by a delicate domed tempietto. Beyond is St Mary's, with its superb spire bursting forth from a scrum of pinnacles. Can a city present a more sublime mellow stone townscape?

OXFORD

Carfax Tower 1922 71997

Things fall off a bit when the High reaches Carfax, at the corner of St Aldate's Street and Cornmarket Street. The medieval Carfax Tower belongs to St Martin's Church, the rest of which was demolished in 1896. Boffin's was replaced in 1931 by a Martin's Bank, now the Abbey National. Beyond, on the left of Queen Street, all has since been replaced.

OXFORD, CORNMARKET STREET 1922 71996
As we turn right along Cornmarket Street, the most striking building amid the shops is the rough-hewn late Anglo-Saxon tower of St Michael's Church, with its two tiers of paired belfry windows. To the right, the tall gabled building of 1915 is still occupied by W H Smith, but there have been some losses on the left side of the street, now partly pedestrianised.

ABINGDON, THE LOCK FROM BELOW 1890   26990

ABINGDON
The Lock from Below 1890
Downstream, you reach the market town of Abingdon, once noted for its important medieval abbey, dissolved in 1538. The monks appear to have diverted the Thames closer to their abbey; much later, Abingdon Lock was formed at the east end of Abbey Meadows in 1790. Since this view was taken, the lock has been reconstructed; the lock-keeper's cottage was rebuilt in 1928 by the Thames Conservancy.

◆

ABINGDON
Abbey Mill 1890
Abingdon Abbey was founded in 675 AD, and the town grew up at its gates. However, nothing remains of its great monastic church. Along Thames Street, east of the town's medieval river bridge, abbey buildings remain. Note the gabled 13th-century chimney stack to The Chequer. The mill, functioning in 1890, is now a house, and the weatherboarded bag-hoist house has gone.

ABINGDON, ABBEY MILL 1890   26992

ABINGDON, THE BOAT HOUSE 1890 26987
We are looking upstream from the centre of the 14th-century stone bridge across the Thames where it crosses Nag's Head Island. The landing stage to the Crown and Thistle, a hotel some way away on Bridge Street, now belongs to The Mill House, the pub on the island. The weatherboarded outbuilding has since been demolished.

ABINGDON, VIEW FROM THE ELMS 1890 26988x
Downstream, this view looks back to the town from the east bank with Nag's Head Island separating the two river channels .The octagonal building on the left is the former gaol, now the Old Gaol Leisure Centre, an austere building of 1805-1811.

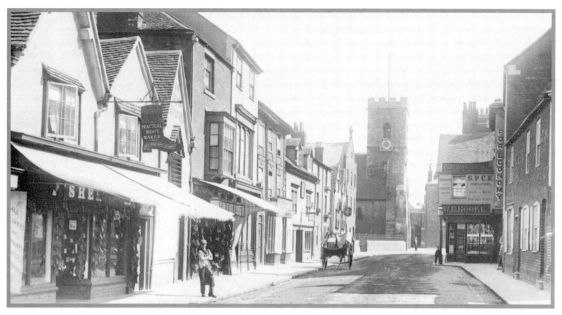

ABINGDON, STERT STREET 1893 31693

Rather unkindly, Jerome K Jerome of 'Three Men in a Boat' fame, and our constant companion along the river from Oxford to Kingston, described Abingdon as 'quiet, eminently respectable, clean and desperately dull'. This view looks along Stert Street towards the tower of St Nicholas Church which faces the Market Place; the street still retains much of its character, apart from the traffic.

ABINGDON, MARKET PLACE 1890 26994

This is very much an archive photograph, for only the bank on the left survives from 1890: Queen Victoria's statue, commemorating her Golden Jubilee of 1887, was moved to the abbey park in 1946, while the gutless Corn Exchange of 1886 and the Queen's Hotel of 1864 were swept away for the awful 1960s Bury Street shopping street.

CULHAM, THE COLLEGE 1900 45208

South-east of Abingdon, on the A415 and a mile west of the Culham Science Centre, the former Culham College is a large and austere Victorian Gothic building based on an Oxford collegiate layout with a quad. It was founded in 1852 by Bishop Samuel Wilberforce as an early teacher training college; it is now the European School, minus the creeper.

SUTTON COURTENAY, THE VILLAGE 1890 27001

This remarkable village has three medieval stone houses, as well as the Norman church whose tower we see in this view. The Swan pub dates from the 1870s and, apart from the loss of the boundary wall and railings, remains, as do the cottages. The green now has more lime trees along its edge and an unusual World War I memorial.

CLIFTON HAMPDEN, THE VILLAGE AND THE CHURCH 1890 27006
This photograph, taken from the east bank of the river, south of the Barley Mow pub, manages to exclude George Gilbert Scott's rather fine 1864 seven-arched brick bridge over the river. At the right, on the ridge, is St Michael and All Angels Church, which owes its picturesqueness to Scott rather than the middle ages.

CLIFTON HAMPDEN, THE BARLEY MOW INN 1890 27010
On the east bank, beyond the bridge, this medieval inn is noted for its 'cruck' construction, the large curved timbers in the gable wall, and for the fact that Jerome K Jerome commends it in 'Three Men in a Boat'. The timbers are now painted black rather than being (correctly) limewashed as in this view. A house is now built behind.

DORCHESTER, THE VILLAGE 1924 76211

Our progress down-river reaches Dorchester. It was a Roman town and the seat of an Anglo-Saxon bishopric, and is now dominated by its great late 11th-century Abbey church. Nowadays the by-passed winding High Street is again peaceful. The cottage on the left has been demolished but the others remain, including the rather fine White Hart Hotel, dated 1691 but in fact earlier, a former coaching inn.

SHILLINGFORD, THE SWAN HOTEL 1890 27018

Now known as the Shillingford Bridge Hotel, and with a large and rather poor extension replacing the clapboarded building to the right, this Georgian inn is situated on the south bank by the elegant bridge of 1826, which was a toll bridge until 1874. The bridge replaced others which in their turn had replaced a ferry.

WALLINGFORD, THE BRIDGE BOAT HOUSE 1899 42988
A little further downstream we reach historic
Wallingford, an Anglo-Saxon borough, much of whose
9th-century earthen ramparts remain. There are the
earthworks also of the Norman castle in the north-east
quarter of the town. Here the old town landing-stage
is north of the bridge; the quay is much altered, with
the boathouse now the Mill House pub.

WALLINGFORD, MARKET PLACE 1893 31712

In Wallingford's town centre is a fine Market Place. The railed enclosure with the lamp post has gone, but the 1885 drinking fountain and canopy, to the right of the 'growler' cab, remain, or rather were reinstated in 1979. The buildings on the left have gone, their replacements dull to awful.

WALLINGFORD, THE CHURCH AND THE BRIDGE 1899 42986

Back on the river, this view looks north-east from the Crowmarsh Gifford bank to Bridge House, with the remarkable spire of St Peter's Church beyond. Designed by the normally staid Sir Robert Taylor, the church is inventive and free Gothic, but of 1777. The bridge is remarkable too, and long, with seventeen arches, three of them medieval, three of 1809 and the rest of 1751.

STREATLEY, FROM STREATLEY DOWNS 1890 27052
Downstream from Wallingford, the Thames cuts the Goring Gap between the Chilterns and the Berkshire Downs. Brunel's Great Western Railway also took advantage of the gap for his route from Paddington to Bristol. In this view from the Downs, we look north over Streatley, which was then in Berkshire: its parish church is on the left, with Goring on the right, across the river.

STREATLEY, THE VILLAGE 1904 52933
Streatley lies at the junction of several major routes as they converge on the Goring Gap. This is now the busy A329, and the B4009 Newbury road is between the Bull at Streatley pub on the left, where the Three Men in a Boat lunched, and the Georgian Elm House beyond. The 'Wells' grocer's sign survives, but the shop is now a living room.

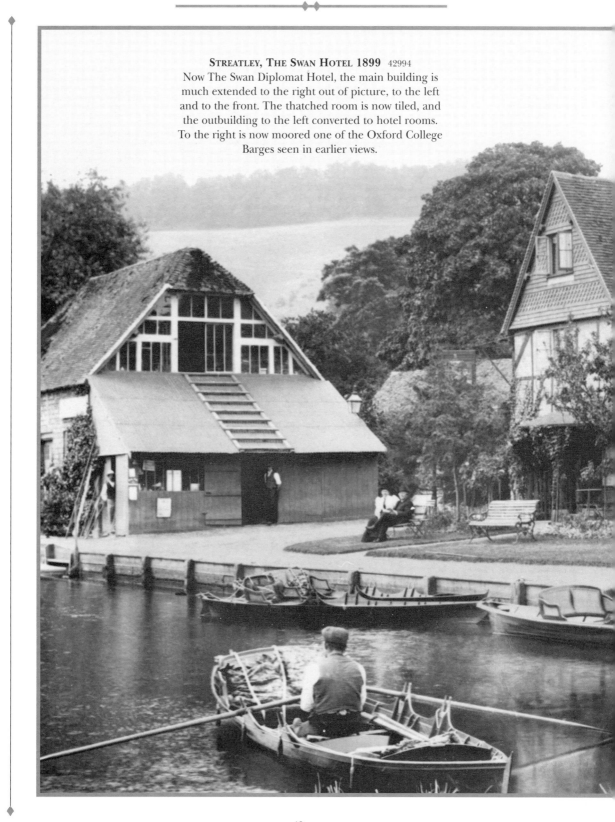

STREATLEY, THE SWAN HOTEL 1899 42994
Now The Swan Diplomat Hotel, the main building is much extended to the right out of picture, to the left and to the front. The thatched room is now tiled, and the outbuilding to the left converted to hotel rooms. To the right is now moored one of the Oxford College Barges seen in earlier views.

STREATLEY, THE LOCK AND WEIR c1955 S221004
Seen from the road bridge, its balustrades recently brutalised by the Oxfordshire County Engineer, the lock, rebuilt in 1922, is little changed, although the Victorian former lock-keeper's cottage is now painted white. The weir has been rebuilt recently.

GORING, THE LOCK 1896 38313
Further along the bridge we look into the backwater with the lock island on the left and the old lock-keeper's cottage beyond the tree. Goring collected a number of late Victorian and Edwardian riverside houses and boathouses between the river and the village proper. The now tiled boathouse on the right is today a doctor's surgery.

GORING, THE VILLAGE 1899 42991
Opposite the well-known Miller of Mansfield hotel and pub, mainly Georgian with older parts, is the Goring Free Church, dated 1893, on the corner of Manor Road, still looking pretty fresh in this view only six years later. Little has changed in this view over the last century, apart from the traffic levels.

PANGBOURNE, WHITCHURCH BRIDGE 1890 27066
The Thames emerges from the Goring Gap at Pangbourne, and the valley widens out again. This view looks downstream from the riverside garden of Waterside House towards Whitchurch Bridge. This late Victorian iron bridge renewed a timber bridge erected in 1792 to replace a ferry, and is one of few surviving toll bridges (cars 10p).

PANGBOURNE, THE SWAN HOTEL 1890 27060

Frith's photographer swivelled his camera, while crossing the little River Pang which reaches the Thames here, and walked a few yards along the bank to capture this view back upstream towards the recently rebuilt weir. The Swan Inn, whose outbuilding close to the weir survives, claims to date back to 1642.

PANGBOURNE, WHITCHURCH LOCK c1955 P5039

The lock is only accessible by water, for it is cut off from Whitchurch by a backwater and house gardens: even the Thames Path misses the river here, only going through the churchyard. This view looks from the lock-keeper's cottage garden eastwards into the lock. The chestnut palings are now a smart well-trimmed beech hedge.

PANGBOURNE, THE VILLAGE 1893 31719

We are in the centre of the village; this view looks north along Church Street with the churchyard wall on the left. Sad to relate, the pines have now gone, and there are pavements to protect pedestrians from the surging traffic. The Cross Keys remains, but the two houses in the distance on either side of the High Street junction are now estate agents.

MAPLEDURHAM, THE LOCK 1890 27089

Moving downstream towards Reading we reach Mapledurham Lock. Although since this view was taken the lock, the footbridge, and the lock-keeper's cottage have all been rebuilt, it is still a tranquil stretch; the steam launch entering the lock may be similar to the one that towed the Three Men in a Boat through on their way upstream to Pangbourne.

MAPLEDURHAM, THE MILL 1890 27091
Mapledurham's old part-Tudor watermill survives; its waterwheel can be seen in this view. Apart from a lean-to added to the front, the building is remarkably unchanged; a lane leads into the superb village with its great Elizabethan mansion.

CAVERSHAM, THE BRIDGE 1904 52027
The Thames flows past Reading. The town centre is closer to the River Kennet, on its way to merge with the main river. Here from the Reading bank we look towards the 1869 iron Caversham bridge; it was demolished in 1924 to be replaced in 1926 by the present concrete one.

CAVERSHAM, THE CHURCH 1913 65923
This view shows the tower of St Peter's Church from the now much-municipalised Reading bank. The church tower was rebuilt in 1878. The mansion to the right amid the trees is Caversham Court, which was demolished in 1933; its 17th-century stable block remains, and the grounds are a most attractive public park.

CAVERSHAM, BRIDGE STREET 1908 59962
The Thames Valley Hotel on the left was built in 1891
and is now flats, while the Crown Hotel on the right was
rebuilt when the present bridge was constructed. The
1869 bridge seen here replaced an odd 18th-century
one: it was made of timber on the Berkshire south side
and stone on the Oxfordshire or Caversham side, owing
to a cross border disagreement.

CAVERSHAM, THE LOCK 1890 27105
Much in this view has changed since 1890: the mid 19th-century lock-keeper's cottage was rebuilt by the Thames Conservancy in 1931 and the area to the left has been built up with industrial buildings and boat repairers, while the lock itself has been substantially altered. To the right across a stream, fine plane trees planted in King's Meadow park now overhang the towpath.

SONNING, THE LOCK 1890 27159
About three miles downstream we reach Sonning Lock, seen here on a tranquil late summer's day. The lock has since been entirely reconstructed, and the lock-keeper's cottage, seen peeping from the trees, was rebuilt in 1916. Note the tall ladder leaning in the apple tree. To the right are the grounds of the Reading Blue Coat School which moved here in 1946.

SONNING, THE BRIDGE 1904 52035
Seen from the footbridge to the Oxfordshire bank, the eleven-arch bridge is an 18th-century one that carries a vast amount of traffic, for Sonning is in effect Reading's eastern by-pass. The Great House Hotel on the left is now much extended, and the church tower is largely concealed by more mature trees.

SONNING, THE VILLAGE 1904 52040
South of Thames Street the through traffic can be avoided. In this view we look down Pearson Street, with the High Street off to the left beyond the cart. The best house in this view is the one with the diagonal chimneystacks, The Grove: it is Tudor, with an 18th-century pink-washed facade and a superb Queen Anne door hood.

SHIPLAKE, THE MILL AND LOCK 1890 27167

As we reach Shiplake Lock, only the lock, albeit entirely reconstructed, survives in this view looking upstream to the lock. The large weatherboarded watermill was demolished around 1900 and only the mill house remained, just off the picture to the right. The waterwheel housing can be seen on the left wall of the mill.

WARGRAVE, FROM NEAR THE FERRY 1890 27173

The ferry has long gone, but this view from the Oxfordshire bank looking north-east captures the river's character well. To the right is the ferry slipway behind the St George and Dragon pub. The central trees hide Wargrave Manor with its parkland; further along the bank there are now a number of larger Edwardian and later houses.

WARGRAVE, THE VILLAGE 1890 27177

The photographer has captured a sleepy Thames-side village just on the point of modernising to meet new demands from the middle classes, who were building along the river and around the villages. A brand new terrace of shops on the left replace some cottages, and soon after 1890 the Greyhound and Burgis' stores were rebuilt more grandly.

HENLEY-ON-THAMES, THE REGATTA 1890 27203

The Henley Royal Regatta has become one of the key social occasions of the year, on a par with Royal Ascot and Wimbledon. Here, seen from near Poplar Point on the Berkshire bank, the eights race past the houseboats which lined the opposite bank to provide elegant floating grandstands for hospitality and shelter from the rain.

HENLEY-ON-THAMES, THE REGATTA 1890 27200
It all started when the Oxford and Cambridge Boat Race was held here in 1829, but the first Regatta proper was held in June 1839. This scene shows the 1890 crowds lining the course, which started at Temple Island in the distance. The Firs on the left, with its oriel window, is at the end of Riverside, now private parking for the hotel.

HENLEY-ON-THAMES, REGATTA DAY 1899 43017

Looking from Henley's superb river bridge of 1786 with keystones carved by Anne Seymour Damer with the heads of Isis and Thames, we see the boathouses at the east end of Riverside, which are still in use, and the houseboat grandstands. There are now two grandstands in the middle distance instead.

HENLEY-ON-THAMES, HART STREET 1893 31733

The photographer walked away from the river bridge up Hart Street towards the Town Hall in Market Place and turned back by the Bell Street junction to take this view towards the church with its dominating earlier 16th-century tower. All the buildings survive today, except for a tall half-timbered Barclays Bank of 1910 inserted on the right hand side.

MARLOW
From the Lock 1890

This view, taken from Lock Island, looks towards the beautiful suspension bridge and the 1832 parish church which replaced the medieval one. This old church had been regularly flooded, particularly after the pound lock was built in 1773, and it partly collapsed in 1831. Here we see the old spire of 1832, a curiously knobbly affair with gigantic crockets.

❖

MARLOW
The Weir 1901

Ten years after photograph No 23672, the church has its brand new spire, completed in 1899. This was designed by John Oldrid Scott, second son of the great Victorian architect, George Gilbert Scott, who built Clifton Hampden's bridge over the Thames further upstream, as well as St Pancras station and the Foreign Office in London.

MARLOW, FROM THE LOCK 1890 23672

MARLOW, THE WEIR 1901 47129

MARLOW, FROM THE LOCK 1901 47125

Marlow, and Henley further up river, were important inland ports handling mainly the corn, malt and timber of the Chiltern Hills behind them. Both are now prosperous middle-class towns, and the ripe language of the former bargees, fishermen and wharfinger inhabitants would not be welcome. This view has been a very popular one with photographers and painters over the years.

MARLOW, THE EMBANKMENT c1955 M35024

Nowadays the bank is more formalised and the trees are fewer than in this view, which looks along the river bank north-east to the suspension bridge. This bridge, by William Tierney Clark, and opened in 1832, so impressed a visiting Hungarian nobleman that Clark was commissioned to built a larger one over the Danube to link Buda and Pest.

MARLOW, THE FISHERMAN'S RETREAT 1890 23690

We end this chapter in St Peter Street, which originally led to the old wooden bridge replaced by the present one further west. The tumbledown cottages, now long gone, were occupied by bargees, wharfingers, brewery labourers and others, while the Fisherman's Retreat, the house with the blinds, was popular with anglers and pleasure boaters, including Jerome K Jerome, who often stayed here.

COOKHAM, ODNEY COMMON 1925 77588

Downstream beyond Marlow the Thames reaches Cookham, where it blunders about and divides into three channels before turning south by chalk cliffs. This view is from Odney Common, an island along the north side of one of the channels, here named Lulle Brook. This view south is little changed, apart from a footbridge in the middle distance.

COOKHAM, THE MILL STREAM 1899 43029

As we look back towards Cookham from near the viewpoint of photograph No 77588 towards the bridge onto Odney, since rebuilt, the Thames is beyond the trees with its two channels. The northern one meanders past Hedsor Wharf, cut off by the Lock Cut of 1830. The Lulle Brook in the view is the third and southernmost channel.

COOKHAM, HIGH STREET 1925 77584

The village main street is little changed, although Bel and the Dragon on the right is no longer also a garage. To the left, just out of view, is the Stanley Spencer Gallery in the old Methodist chapel of 1846. This quirky artist is Cookham's famous son, being born at Fernlea further down the High Street in 1891 and buried in the churchyard.

MAIDENHEAD, THE FERRY AND THE COTTAGE 1906 54103

Past Cliveden is one of the most beautiful stretches of the Thames with its tree-clad river cliffs. Here, a little south of Cookham, is the My Lady Ferry with the lock-keeper's cottage on the far bank. Now defunct, it originally carried barge-towing horses to the opposite towpath; later it became more of a leisure ferry to Cliveden House on the plateau above.

MAIDENHEAD, BOULTERS LOCK BRIDGE 1906 54082

The artist Edward Gregory's famous painting 'Boulters Lock, Sunday Afternoon' superbly captured the cheerful, crowded chaos of a summer weekend, even featuring himself lounging in a boat. Starting it in 1882, he finished it only in 1897. He lived his last few years in Marlow, further upstream, and is buried in its churchyard.

MAIDENHEAD, BOULTERS LOCK 1906 54083

This Edwardian view at one of the Thames' most famous locks captures well the increasing affluence of the middle and lower middle classes; they flocked out of London in their thousands onto the river at weekends, hiring punts, skiffs, rowing boats, sailing boats and steam launches by the score. On Ascot Sunday 1888 over 800 boats and 72 steam launches passed through the lock.

MAIDENHEAD, BOULTERS LOCK 1913 65542
A little later, the year before the First World War started, the great boating craze of the later Victorian and Edwardian years is still in full swing. According to Jerome K Jerome, the oarsmen and punters loathed the steam launches and went out of their way to annoy them: this would mean an uneasy truce in the confines of the lock.

MAIDENHEAD, BOULTERS LOCK 1913 65543
The lock, first built in 1830 to cope with the six foot fall in the river, was rebuilt in 1912, the year before this view was taken. It has subsequently been rebuilt again, but the more elaborate balustered bridge of 1912 remains, replacing the one featured in Gregory's painting. The lock-keeper's cottage was partly rebuilt in 2000.

MAIDENHEAD, BOULTERS LOCK, THE ELEVATOR 1913 65545
These elevators were installed at a number of busy locks to cope with the vast numbers of small leisure boats spawned by the boating craze these views capture. The wooden elevator ramps have now long gone, but their concrete runways remain. The bridge has been rebuilt; on the right is the Boulters Lock Hotel, which is still thriving.

MAIDENHEAD, BRIDGE STREET 1890 23633

Poor old Maidenhead: a rather good Georgian coaching town on the old London to Bath road, it was overlaid by Victorian development after the railway arrived in 1841, and has really suffered from ring road and redevelopment mania in the 1960s. Here, looking towards the town centre, very little survives. The pub on the right, now Anthonia's Bistro, is one of few surviving reference points.

MAIDENHEAD, HIGH STREET 1911 63797

Here we see the flat-fronted Georgian buildings interspersed with Victorian and Edwardian ones that gave Maidenhead a distinctive character. The turreted and lead domed building of 1903, now Dorothy Perkins, survives, but the left hand one was replaced by a nine-storey monster office block, Berkshire House, and others were swept away in the vandalistic 1960s.

MAIDENHEAD, THE BRIDGE 1906 54099

Half a mile downstream the river passes through Sir Robert Taylor's supremely graceful and beautiful sandstone bridge of the 1770s that still carries the busy A4 London to Bath road. For once, the balustraded parapets have not been interfered with by over-zealous highway engineers, as at Staines. The buildings on the right have been replaced by 1990s blocks of flats.

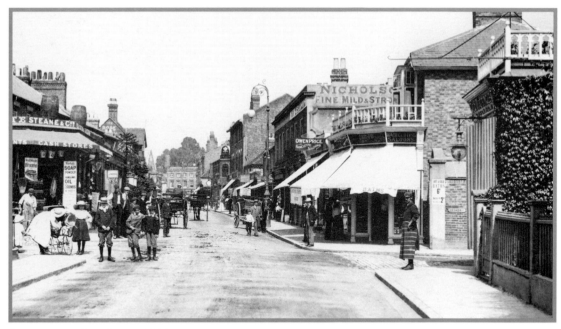

MAIDENHEAD, KING STREET 1904 52372

The north end of King Street has changed dramatically since 1904: the right hand side is mostly occupied by the backside of Tesco's, and on the left only The Rose pub, with the tall chimney, and the Methodist Church of 1859 beyond remain. This once busy road led to the Great Western Railway station further south.

WINDSOR, THE CASTLE FROM THE RIVER 1895 35368A

Frith's photographer could not resist one of the most photographed views along the Thames: Windsor Castle on its cliff-top towering above the town and river. The largest continuously inhabited medieval castle in the world, it covers thirteen acres. However, much of what we see now owes more to the 1820s; at that time George IV expended the then fabulous sum of £1,000,000.

WINDSOR, CASTLE HILL 1914 66981

Queen Victoria's Golden Jubilee statue of 1887 replaced a market cross, and emphasises the 'company town' nature of Royal Windsor, for the castle has been a royal residence since 1075. The keep (with the flagpole) was raised to three storeys and the outer walls and towers refaced in the 1820s: the walls still look remarkably fresh in 2000.

ETON, COLLEGE BARNES POOL 1923 74801

On the Buckinghamshire bank (since 1974 in Berkshire) Henry VI's great foundation, Eton College, has rendered this another 'company town'. Behind the hipped roofs of Corner House loom the pinnacles of Eton College chapel, built between 1449 and 1483. The morning-coated and top-hatted scholars stroll past Barnes Pool, rebuilt in 1930 in Neo-Georgian style.

ETON, FOURTH OF JUNE PROCESSION OF BOATS 1906 53724
Back at the river, this view shows the crowds watching the Procession of
College Boats, held every year on 4 June to commemorate George III's
birthday. The king took a keen interest in the College, and often crossed
the bridge to talk to scholars. The Etonians and their guests here throng
the Eton bank: toppers, Eton collars and ladies' floral hats aplenty.

WINDSOR, RIVERSIDE GARDENS 1906 53721

On the Windsor bank the non-Etonian spectators watch the Procession of College Boats. In the distance, lined with spectators, is the bridge, nowadays pedestrianised. There was a timber bridge here by 1172, but the present one with cast-iron spans dates from 1821. These Riverside Gardens have been reduced to a narrow stone walled strip to accommodate a widened Barry Avenue.

WINDSOR, ROMNEY LOCK 1906 53722

A little further downstream, Romney Lock gives excellent views of Eton College across the river. The lock has since been reconstructed and the lock-keeper's cottage was rebuilt in 1919. The Thames Path reaches the lock from Windsor via Romney Walk, sandwiched between the river and the railway which arrived at Windsor as a branch line in 1850.

STAINES, BELL WEIR LOCK 1907 58000

Below Old Windsor, the river reaches Runnymede, where in 1215 on an island now named Magna Carta Island, King John signed the great charter, widely regarded as the foundation of English liberty. Past it is Bell Weir Lock, now reconstructed, as is the weir on the right: it used to have a pitched roof structure to protect the weir machinery.

STAINES, THE BRIDGE 1907 57990

This view looks downstream from the Egham bank. The refined and somewhat austere rusticated three-arch bridge of 1829-32 by John Rennie, the architect of old Waterloo Bridge, has been marred by a widening in 1958 in which footways were cantilevered from each side and Rennie's simple solid parapets replaced by skinny railings. The ABC cinema now fills the skyline above the left hand arch.

STAINES, VIEW FROM THE BRIDGE 1907 57991
As we pass beneath the bridge, still on the Egham bank, the 18th-century Swan Hotel on the right now also occupies the boathouse and garage in front of it, behind the ladies with their parasols. On the left is the roof of Staines' Town Hall, a dull building dated 1880. The chimney and works of William Ridley and Sons has now gone.

STAINES, THE RIVER 1907 57993
A little further downstream, just through the railway bridge, the view down river from the Staines bank has changed; now there is extensive housing development on both banks, much fortunately still hidden by riverside trees. The fences on the left belong to the back gardens of houses in Laleham Road, a Victorian and Edwardian expansion of the town.

STAINES, HIGH STREET 1907 57995

Staines was formerly in Middlesex. It is an ancient town with a medieval layout and a wide gently curving High Street, now mainly pedestrianised. Most of the right hand side has been rebuilt, but The Angel on the left survives (albeit with fake timber-framing), as does the tall twin-gabled building next to it of 1873. Beyond, survival is more patchy.

WALTON-ON-THAMES, THE ANGLERS 1908 60037

As Jerome K Jerome observed, 'only the tiniest corner of it (Walton on Thames) comes down to the river'. Here, as we look downstream by the former ferry and towpath, working barges mingle with leisure rowing boats for hire. Beyond is the Swan's garden, then boathouses (now the Boathouse Gallery); the sheds have been replaced by The Anglers pub, probably built about 1910.

WALTON-ON-THAMES
The Boathouse 1899
Downstream, past Weybridge, the Desborough Cut of 1935 by-passes a winding loop, to reach Walton-on-Thames. Beyond Walton Bridge is this boathouse and its harbour inlet off the river, here charmingly informal. It is now Walton Marina, with an emphasis on cabin cruisers rather than punts. The building survives, clad in plastic weatherboarding, but the banks have been sheet-piled and denuded of trees.

◆

TEDDINGTON
The Bridge 1899
As every schoolchild knows (or used to), the tidal Thames finishes at Teddington. The main river is crossed by this spindly-looking suspension bridge of 1888, seen here from the lock island. To the left of The Anglers, out of view, are the famous Teddington TV Studios, while the boathouse to the right is the home of the British Motor Yacht Club.

WALTON-ON-THAMES, THE BOATHOUSE 1899   43040

TEDDINGTON, THE BRIDGE 1899   43051

TEDDINGTON, THE LOCK AND THE ROLLERS 1899 43054
Seen from the north end of the lock island are the boat rollers, now disused, then the narrow skiff lock, nicknamed 'The Coffin', and then a further two locks, both now rebuilt. The main lock is vast, 650 feet long, and designed to accommodate eight Thames barges and a steam tug. A footbridge carries pedestrians across the lock.

TWICKENHAM, FROM THE ISLAND BOAT HOUSE 1890 23534
This and photograph No 23535 are taken from Eel Pie Island, apparently named after the famous pies sold at the Island Tavern. Here the photographer looks towards St Mary's 14th-century church tower, with the triangular pediment of the Georgian nave, designed in 1714 by John James, to its right. The church is now more visible, for the house in front has since been demolished.

TWICKENHAM, KING STREET 1909 T91001
This view of King Street looks east towards the grand
Portland stone bank at its end. Built as the London and
Provincial Bank, this Palladian-style Edwardian building
is now a Barclays Bank; it is more visible now, as the
right hand buildings were demolished and rebuilt
further back to allow King Street to be widened.

TWICKENHAM, THE ISLAND 1890 23535

This view, from the footbridge onto the Island, is a photograph of what has passed - for all to the left of the sash-windowed and pedimented house on the right was cleared away in the 1950s. To get your bearings, the road behind the slipway is Water Lane. It is regrettable that little of coherence or merit has replaced any of it.

RICHMOND, MESSUMS BOATYARD 1899 43741

As we approach Richmond, this view from the west bank looks towards the Petersham Road across to the former Messum's Boatyard. All survives, including the terrace of boathouses and the central building, now reduced to two storeys by the removal of the weatherboarded upper storey; it is now the Richmond Canoe Club. The gabled Three Pigeons to its right is now derelict.

RICHMOND, FROM THE BRIDGE 1899 43739

Beyond the scrum of pleasure boats for hire in this view looking downstream from Richmond Bridge is the three-storeyed White Cross pub. The area between the White Cross and the photographer is now occupied by Richmond Riverside, a splendid collection of 1980s Georgian-style office blocks by Quinlan Terry above a zig-zag of ramped terraces down to the embankment.

RICHMOND, THE BRIDGE 1890 23544

Looking back upstream past the boathouses in front of the 1830s St Helena Terrace and The White Cross, we see a fine view of Richmond Bridge, which dates from the 1770s and is one of the Thames' finest Georgian bridges. Beyond the bridge the skyline is now dominated by the vast Neo-Georgian Star and Garter Home for disabled ex-servicemen, built in 1921.

RICHMOND, THREE BRIDGES 1899 43738

Downstream from the town, the photographer looks back to the Richmond Half-Tide Weir and Footbridge. There are boat rollers by the Isleworth bank on the right, and Richmond Lock is on the left. This and the stylish pedestrian bridge date from 1892-4. Between this and the 1848 railway bridge beyond is now Twickenham Bridge of 1930, in effect the Richmond by-pass.

KEW GARDENS 1899 43757

Between Richmond and Kew, on the Surrey bank, are the three hundred acres of the Royal Botanical Gardens, opened to the public in 1841. Besides the botanical collections there are a number of superb buildings, including Sir William Chambers' Chinese Pagoda of 1761 and Decimus Burton's stupendous Palm House of the 1840s, which is 360 feet long and partly 62 feet high. It is astonishingly simple and pure architecture for its date.

HAMMERSMITH, THE BRIDGE c1965 H387019

The Thames is now flowing into London proper, and we reach Hammersmith, with its monumentally-scaled iron bridge. This replaced William Tierney Clark's suspension bridge of 1827, a smaller version of which survives across the Thames at Marlow. The current one, now painted a tasteful green with architectural ornament picked out in gold, is by Sir Joseph Bazalgette and is dated 1887.

HAMMERSMITH, THE BRIDGE c1965 H387014

We meet Bazalgette later at the Embankment in central London; seen here from the Barnes bank towpath, his suspension bridge has a 420-foot main span, and the towers are finished with French-style pavilion roofs, all in sheet iron. Beyond the left tower are the tower blocks of the Queen Caroline Estate, and to the right the BBC's Riverside Studios.

HAMMERSMITH, THE PIER c1965 H387003

The photographer looks west from Hammersmith Bridge along Lower Mall, a good jumble of 18th-, 19th- and 20th-century building, including the well-known Doves pub. Beyond the pier is Upper Mall where William Morris lived from 1878 to 1896, naming his Georgian terrace house, number 26, Kelmscott House after his country house in Oxfordshire.

LONDON, CHELSEA 1890 L130084

Further along the north bank the Thames passes Chelsea's Cheyne Walk. The pavilion roofs on the right were once Lindsey House of 1684, subsequently owned by the Moravian Sect, who added the French mansard roofs. In 1774 it was subdivided into five houses. Bomb damage removed the buildings left of the white stucco, which were to be replaced by the Cremorne Estate in the 1950s.

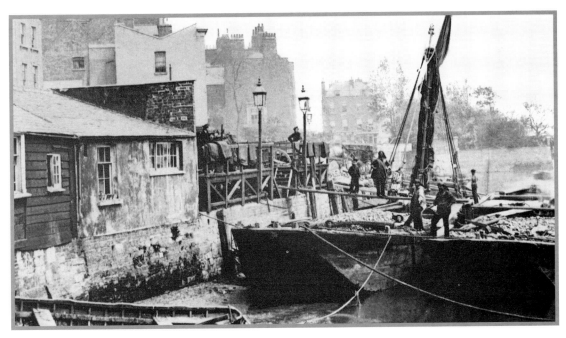

LONDON, CHELSEA EMBANKMENT 1890 L130091

This is a much changed view: the working barges have gone, to be replaced by ranks of houseboats. The buildings in the foreground and the far left have gone, although the mansard roof of Lindsey House can be seen beyond the stuccoed M-roof. This area is now part of the Chelsea Embankment, part of which opened in 1874.

LONDON, CHELSEA EMBANKMENT 1890 L130083

LONDON
Chelsea Embankment 1890
This is an evocative view of a long-dead Chelsea, with sailing vessels moored along the Embankment, one apparently with a cargo of hay. These types of boats have now been replaced by the brightly painted houseboats which are so characteristic of the Chelsea scene.

◆

LONDON
The Houses of Parliament c1890
Further down the Thames are the Houses of Parliament - or rather, the Palace of Westminster. This replaced the old palace, which burned down in 1834. The major difference between then and now are the then heaving commercial wharves and warehouses coming right up to the foot of the Victoria Tower: these produced interesting smells in summer, no doubt.

LONDON, THE HOUSES OF PARLIAMENT c1890 L130277

LONDON, THE HOUSES OF PARLIAMENT 1908 L130149
By this time the wharves have been cleared away to create Victoria Embankment Garden, a more fitting context for the Mother of Parliaments, rebuilt in Gothic style between 1839 and 1860 by Pugin and Sir Charles Barry. Beyond Victoria Tower is the great royal abbey, Westminster Abbey, with its pair of west towers and the centrepiece of the medieval palace, along with Westminster Hall.

LONDON, WESTMINSTER BRIDGE, THE DIAMOND JUBILEE PROCESSION 1897 L130219
This remarkable and historic view from high on the Houses of Parliament shows Queen Victoria's open landau leading the procession across Westminster Bridge. All the buildings on the Lambeth side have gone: County Hall, begun in 1912, is now a Marriott Hotel and aquarium, and to the left is the London Eye, the giant ferris wheel for the Millennium.

LONDON, THE HOUSES OF PARLIAMENT 1890 L130162
From the south bank, near Westminster Bridge, completed
in 1862, this view shows the bell tower known universally by
its great bell, Big Ben. To the right of the bridge, the steep-
roofed buildings have recently been replaced by
architecturally exciting MPs offices; to the right is now
Norman Shaw's 1890-1906 New Scotland Yard, with its
tourelles and brick and stone bands.

LONDON, THAMES EMBANKMENT 1890 L130189

Moving east, this view looks along the Embankment from Charing Cross Bridge to Cleopatra's Needle, an Egyptian obelisk of 1500 BC, given to Britain in 1819 by the Viceroy of Egypt, but only erected here in 1878 following a hair-raising sea voyage. The Savoy Hotel is to its left, which opened the previous year.

LONDON, WATERLOO BRIDGE 1895 L130052

Apart from the wintry ice of a semi-frozen Thames, this view from Savoy Pier shows the old Waterloo Bridge, which was designed by Sir John Rennie and completed in 1817. It was a bridge of great beauty, with pairs of Greek Doric columns to each pier. Unfortunately, in 1936 it was demolished, to be replaced by the present elegant concrete bridge completed in 1942.

LONDON, THE EMBANKMENT FROM TEMPLE PIER 1890 L130077

The Embankment, with its dolphin lampposts dated 1870, is by Bazalgette; in fact it hides the great sewers he built to collect London's effluent and take it further east to rid the city of its appalling cholera epidemics and other diseases - previously the effluent was discharged directly into the Thames. Bazalgette also designed the Temple Pier and its arch of 1868.

LONDON, BLACKFRIARS BRIDGE 1890 L130070

Taken from the Southwark side, this photograph gives a fine view of St Paul's Cathedral, Sir Christopher Wren's Baroque masterpiece (1675-1711) which replaced the medieval cathedral destroyed in the Great Fire of 1666. Nowadays, to the left beyond the cathedral are the tower blocks of the Barbican, completed in 1981. Blackfriars Bridge, dated 1869, screens the now part-demolished railway bridge of 1864.

LONDON, LONDON BRIDGE c1880 L1303429
Further east is yet another bridge by John Rennie, this time father and son. Completed in 1831, it replaced the 12th-century one of nursery rhyme fame, which had only had its houses finally removed in 1762 and lasted for over six centuries. Demolished in 1968, this London Bridge was re-erected in the USA at Lake Huvasu City in Arizona.

LONDON, ST PAUL'S CATHEDRAL 1890 L130126

From the south bank the photographer looks across to Queenhithe dock. Although the river bank is relatively unchanged, all the riverside buildings have gone, the last only in 1996. Beyond is the noble dome of St Paul's Cathedral, while behind the photographer Shakespeare's Globe Theatre has recently been entirely reconstructed, and the massive Bankside Power Station of 1960 is being converted for the Tate Gallery.

LONDON, LONDON BRIDGE 1904 L130178

Here the 1903 widening of the bridge has just been completed, hence the pristine stonework. All to the left on the north bank, apart from the grand pedimented and columned Fishmongers Hall of 1831 near the bridge, has now gone. To the right the tower of Wren's St Magnus the Martyr, and The Monument, erected where the Great Fire of 1666 started, are glimpsed between later office blocks.

LONDON, THE TOWER OF LONDON c1955 L1305022
As we look from Tower Bridge, the dominance of William the Conqueror's White Tower keep, dating from the late 11th century and still the focus of the castle, is now somewhat reduced by office blocks, including the 600 foot high 1970s NatWest Tower and the bizarre 1980s Minster Court. The other tower in this view is the former Port of London Authority building, Edwardian Baroque completed in 1922.

LONDON, THE OPENING OF TOWER BRIDGE 1894 L130019
The bridge was authorised by Act of Parliament in 1885 and opened in 1894. The bascules carrying the roadway are in their fully raised position to allow tall-masted ships and sailing barges to pass through, giving a clearance of 140 feet and a width of 200 feet. The boats dressed overall with signal flags have just passed through.

LONDON, TOWER BRIDGE UNDER CONSTRUCTION 1890 L130050
This murky view looks west from the Pool of London towards what was to become one
of the mechanical wonders of the late 19th century. Here we see the towers - 'steel
skeletons clothed in stone' as described by Sir John Wolfe Barry, the architect - not yet
stone clad, and the upper walkway taking shape.

LONDON, TOWER BRIDGE 1896 L130519

The bustling wharves include Billingsgate on the left, and show why the Tower Bridge design was necessary for masted ships to gain access to this part of the river. Nowadays the biggest ship hereabouts is the light cruiser HMS 'Belfast', a floating World War II museum, moored on the right hand side, while the bridge opens relatively rarely.

LONDON, TOWER BRIDGE 1910 L130058

This photograph was taken from the west. Tower Bridge has become a virtual symbol of London, and it is certainly a very striking and remarkable structure. There are lifts in the towers, for the original idea was for pedestrians to use the high level footways when the bridge was raised by hydraulic machinery. Fascinating technically to civil engineers, the bridge is beautiful to look at for the rest of us.

LONDON, THAMES SHIPBUILDING c1910 L130056

This chapter opens with some views of a long-lost industrial Thames. Here we see workers arriving by boat at one of the ship-building yards that once dotted the eastern banks; these included the great Millwall Yards, which launched among others Brunel's 'Great Eastern' in 1857. In crisis by 1900, the last yards closed a couple of years after this view was taken.

LONDON, OLD FERRY WHARF 1890 L130085

All along the Thames, and described powerfully by Charles Dickens, houses, inns and tenements tottered and decayed in places such as Deptford, Wapping and Shadwell. Those that survive are now very expensive and desirable riverside houses, and a far cry from their squalid past. You can get an idea of a (non-squalid) riverside house by visiting the Prospect of Whitby pub in Wapping.

LONDON, THE DOCKS c1965 L1305174

The port of London held the absolute key to Britain's stupendous 19th-century industrial wealth. From 1799 onwards the docks east of the Tower of London were dug, becoming one of the industrial wonders of the world and a tourist attraction! Here we see the docks near the end of their life; closures started soon after, with the last docks closing in 1981.

LONDON, THAMES WHARF 1910 L130057

Besides the vast acreage of excavated docks, there were numerous riverside wharfs, from the grandeur of Hay's Wharf near London Bridge to this rather less grand one near the west entrance to the Royal Victoria Dock. All contributed to make London the busiest port in the world: this era is long past, for now Docklands is all smart housing, flats and offices, symbolically dominated by the 850-foot-high Canary Wharf office tower.

ERITH, THE THAMES c1955 E58022

Moving into the Thames Estuary, the river passes Erith, a much rebuilt and rather forlorn remnant with its medieval church of St John the Baptist; the town is now joined by development inland to Bexley. Here in the 1950s ships still pass on their way to and from the Port of London; this view is from the William Corey Promenade, as it is now called, close to the High Street.

GRAVESEND, HMS 'GLEANER' 1902 49043

Anchored off Gravesend is the torpedo gunboat HMS 'Gleaner', built at Sheerness Dockyard in 1890 and sold off in 1905; by that time the faster torpedo boat destroyer, later abbreviated to destroyer, had superceded it. Sheerness, founded in 1665, closed in 1960, and Chatham Dockyards, founded in the 16th century, in 1984, finally severing the Royal Navy's connection with the Thames Estuary.

GRAVESEND, THE PARADE 1902 49042
We are keeping to the Kent bank of the Thames Estuary as the river reaches Gravesend, beyond the Queen Elizabeth II Bridge at Dartford. The town is now greatly expanded inland, but the core of this ancient port is still recognisable around the two piers and the Georgian parish church. Here, in a view now much changed, the photographer looks east towards the town piers and jetties.

GRAVESEND, THE FERRY 1902 49044
Gravesend has two Victorian piers: the Royal Terrace Pier of 1843 lies to the east of the slightly later Town Pier we see in this view. Reached via a cobbled yard in front of The Three Saws pub, and visually obstructed by the high sea wall, the pier is somewhat run down, unlike the Royal Terrace Pier. The Wealdway long distance footpath now starts here.

SHEERNESS, THE ESPLANADE AND BEACH C1955 S528048
East of Gravesend, near where the Thames Estuary meets the North Sea, is Sheerness, a port and seaside resort on the north-west corner of the Isle of Sheppey. Here the funfair and amusement park buildings have been replaced by a new Amusement Park and, behind, a Tesco's, while the sea embankment has also been rebuilt and raised.

GRAYS, THE DARTFORD TUNNEL 1963 G85045
We are now on the north or Essex bank of the Thames Estuary. This rather quaint view shows the then 'up to the minute' toll booths of the newly-opened Dartford Tunnel. Since then and the completion of the M25, the twin tunnels are one way; vehicles crossing from the Essex side use the graceful Queen Elizabeth II suspension bridge which soars above the river.

GRAYS, THE RIVER c1955 G85032
This view captures well the character of much of the Thames estuary: a somewhat bleak, flat shoreline and a smudge of distant chalk hills on the Kent side. Shipping in the roads lies off a somewhat forlorn Grays riverside park, complete with a boating pool and, here, a few benches; along all the estuary, high concrete flood barrier walls now obstruct long views.

GRAYS, THE LIGHTSHIP C1955 G85034

Grays is a much re-developed town, but it has a fine Norman church. South of the town, a long-redundant lightship lies on the slipway near Argent Street; its light was hauled up to the masthead on cables. It is remarkable that it still survives, albeit moved a hundred yards west to the other side of the Thurrock Yacht Club, where it continues to moulder gently on the beach.

TILBURY, THE FERRY C1960 T114027

A little further east along the Essex shore our photographer reaches Tilbury and continues his maritime theme; he firmly turned his back on the remarkable 1670s Tilbury Fort, built by a Dutch engineer to defend the Thames against his own countrymen and the French. Here, the Neo-Georgian harbour buildings with their cupola are seen beyond the landing stages.

TILBURY, THE FERRY c1960 T114001

Sir Edwin Cooper designed the landing stage, baggage halls and offices in the late 1920s; the end of them can be seen on the left. The current Gravesend ferry sails from the right quay, and the harbour buildings are now the London International Cruise Terminal; the great modern container port that supplanted the London Docks are to the west.

SOUTHEND, THE BEACH 1898 40912

There are still remnants of Southend's more select era when it became a fashionable seaside resort after 1791: Royal Terrace and the Royal Hotel, for example. The railway arrived in the 1850s, and Southend expanded rapidly. This view captures its earlier atmosphere, including bathing machines; the gigantic, coarse Palace Hotel of 1901 behind the pier had not yet been built.

SOUTHEND, THE PIER 1898 41377
Southend is proud of its pier, which is over a mile long and has its own railway. The pier opened in 1889, but lost these rather elegant buildings in the 1920s for stylised Art Deco ones. The pier is now flanked by large areas of reclaimed land on which sit a brash funfair and amusement park, Peter Pan's Adventure Island.

SOUTHEND, THE BEACH 1898 40911
Much of this view looking west from the pier is now dry land occupied by the west part of Adventure Island, while Never Never Land lies amid the now much thinned trees on the right. Southend was immensely popular with the lower middle and working classes from north and East London: none of the genteel pretensions of an Eastbourne here.

SOUTHEND, THE SEAFRONT 1898 41382
This view looks east from the pier: excursion sailing boats are waiting for trade. Several of the mid and later 19th-century stucco terrace buildings remain, interspersed with garish work like the Electric Avenue 1990s revamp. Further east is The Kursaal of 1902 with a big dome. The foreground is now the east part of Peter Pan's Adventure Island amusement park.

SHOEBURYNESS, WEST BEACH c1955 S275007
East of Southend, the Thames meets the North Sea at Shoeburyness and its long journey ends. Here, on a sunny 1950s summer's day, the shingle West Beach is crowded; in the distance is Southend and its pier. The view is now changed, with 1960s tower blocks of flats on the skyline. Shoeburyness is now the eastern part of a 'Greater Southend'.

Index

Frith Book Co Titles

Frith Book Company publish over a 100 new titles each year. For latest catalogue please contact Frith Book Co.

Town Books 96pp, 100 photos. County and Themed Books 128pp, 150 photos (unless specified) All titles hardback laminated case and jacket except those indicated pb (paperback)

Around Barnstaple	1-85937-084-5	£12.99		Sheffield and S Yorkshire	1-85937-070-5	£14.99
Around Blackpool	1-85937-049-7	£12.99		Shropshire	1-85937-083-7	£14.99
Around Bognor Regis	1-85937-055-1	£12.99		Staffordshire	1-85937-047-0 (96pp)	£12.99
Around Bristol	1-85937-050-0	£12.99		Suffolk	1-85937-074-8	£14.99
Around Cambridge	1-85937-092-6	£12.99		Surrey	1-85937-081-0	£14.99
Cheshire	1-85937-045-4	£14.99		Around Torbay	1-85937-063-2	£12.99
Around Chester	1-85937-090-X	£12.99		Wiltshire	1-85937-053-5	£14.99
Around Chesterfield	1-85937-071-3	£12.99		Around Bakewell	1-85937-113-2	£12.99
Around Chichester	1-85937-089-6	£12.99		Around Bournemouth	1-85937-067-5	£12.99
Cornwall	1-85937-054-3	£14.99		Cambridgeshire	1-85937-086-1	£14.99
Cotswolds	1-85937-099-3	£14.99		Essex	1-85937-082-9	£14.99
Around Derby	1-85937-046-2	£12.99		Around Great Yarmouth		
Devon	1-85937-052-7	£14.99			1-85937-085-3	£12.99
Dorset	1-85937-075-6	£14.99		Hertfordshire	1-85937-079-9	£14.99
Dorset Coast	1-85937-062-4	£14.99		Isle of Wight	1-85937-114-0	£14.99
Around Dublin	1-85937-058-6	£12.99		Around Lincoln	1-85937-111-6	£12.99
East Anglia	1-85937-059-4	£14.99		Oxfordshire	1-85937-076-4	£14.99
Around Eastbourne	1-85937-061-6	£12.99		Around Shrewsbury	1-85937-110-8	£12.99
English Castles	1-85937-078-0	£14.99		South Devon Coast	1-85937-107-8	£14.99
Around Falmouth	1-85937-066-7	£12.99		Around Stratford upon Avon		
Hampshire	1-85937-064-0	£14.99			1-85937-098-5	£12.99
Isle of Man	1-85937-065-9	£14.99		West Midlands	1-85937-109-4	£14.99
Around Maidstone	1-85937-056-X	£12.99				
North Yorkshire	1-85937-048-9	£14.99				
Around Nottingham	1-85937-060-8	£12.99				
Around Penzance	1-85937-069-1	£12.99				
Around Reading	1-85937-087-X	£12.99				
Around St Ives	1-85937-068-3	£12.99				
Around Salisbury	1-85937-091-8	£12.99				
Around Scarborough	1-85937-104-3	£12.99				
Scottish Castles	1-85937-077-2	£14.99				
Around Sevenoaks and Tonbridge	1-85937-057-8	£12.99				

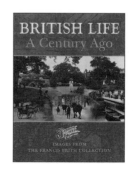

British Life A Century Ago
246 x 189mm
144pp, hardback.
Black and white
Lavishly illustrated with photos from the turn of the century, and with extensive commentary. It offers a unique insight into the social history and heritage of bygone Britain.

1-85937-103-5 £17.99

Available from your local bookshop or from the publisher

Around Bath	1-85937-097-7	£12.99	Mar
County Durham	1-85937-123-x	£14.99	Mar
Cumbria	1-85937-101-9	£14.99	Mar
Down the Thames	1-85937-121-3	£14.99	Mar
Around Exeter	1-85937-126-4	£12.99	Mar
Greater Manchester	1-85937-108-6	£14.99	Mar
Around Guildford	1-85937-117-5	£12.99	Mar
Around Harrogate	1-85937-112-4	£12.99	Mar
Around Leicester	1-85937-073-x	£12.99	Mar
Around Liverpool	1-85937-051-9	£12.99	Mar
Around Newark	1-85937-105-1	£12.99	Mar
Northumberland and Tyne & Wear			
	1-85937-072-1	£14.99	Mar
Around Oxford	1-85937-096-9	£12.99	Mar
Around Plymouth	1-85937-119-1	£12.99	Mar
Around Southport	1-85937-106-x	£12.99	Mar
Welsh Castles	1-85937-120-5	£14.99	Mar
Around Belfast	1-85937-094-2	£12.99	Apr
Canals and Waterways	1-85937-129-9	£17.99	Apr
Down the Severn	1-85937-118-3	£14.99	Apr
East Sussex	1-85937-130-2	£14.99	Apr
Exmoor	1-85937-132-9	£14.99	Apr
Gloucestershire	1-85937-102-7	£14.99	Apr
Around Horsham	1-85937-127-2	£12.99	Apr
Around Ipswich	1-85937-133-7	£12.99	Apr
Ireland (pb)	1-85937-181-7	£9.99	Apr
Kent Living Memories	1-85937-125-6	£14.99	Apr
London (pb)	1-85937-183-3	£9.99	Apr
New Forest	1-85937-128-0	£14.99	Apr
Scotland (pb)	1-85937-182-5	£9.99	Apr
Around Southampton	1-85937-088-8	£12.99	Apr
Stone Circles & Ancient Monuments			
	1-85937-143-4	£17.99	Apr
Sussex (pb)	1-85937-184-1	£9.99	Apr
Colchester (pb)	1-85937-188-4	£8.99	May
County Maps of Britain			
	1-85937-156-6 (192pp)	£19.99	May
Leicestershire (pb)	1-85937-185-x	£9.99	May

Lincolnshire	1-85937-135-3	£14.99	May
Around Newquay	1-85937-140-x	£12.99	May
Nottinghamshire (pb)	1-85937-187-6	£9.99	May
Redhill to Reigate	1-85937-137-x	£12.99	May
Victorian & Edwardian Yorkshire			
	1-85937-154-x	£14.99	May
Around Winchester	1-85937-139-6	£12.99	May
Yorkshire (pb)	1-85937-186-8	£9.99	May
Berkshire (pb)	1-85937-191-4	£9.99	Jun
Brighton (pb)	1-85937-192-2	£8.99	Jun
Dartmoor	1-85937-145-0	£14.99	Jun
East London	1-85937-080-2	£14.99	Jun
Glasgow (pb)	1-85937-190-6	£8.99	Jun
Kent (pb)	1-85937-189-2	£9.99	Jun
Victorian & Edwardian Kent			
	1-85937-149-3	£14.99	Jun
North Devon Coast	1-85937-146-9	£14.99	Jun
Peak District	1-85937-100-0	£14.99	Jun
Around Truro	1-85937-147-7	£12.99	Jun
Victorian & Edwardian Maritime Album			
	1-85937-144-2	£17.99	Jun
West Sussex	1-85937-148-5	£14.99	Jun
Churches of Berkshire	1-85937-170-1	£17.99	Jul
Churches of Dorset	1-85937-172-8	£17.99	Jul
Churches of Hampshire	1-85937-207-4	£17.99	Jul
Churches of Wiltshire	1-85937-171-x	£17.99	Jul
Derbyshire (pb)	1-85937-196-5	£9.99	Jul
Edinburgh (pb)	1-85937-193-0	£8.99	Jul
Herefordshire	1-85937-174-4	£14.99	Jul
Norwich (pb)	1-85937-194-9	£8.99	Jul
Ports and Harbours	1-85937-208-2	£17.99	Jul
Somerset and Avon	1-85937-153-1	£14.99	Jul
South Devon Living Memories			
	1-85937-168-x	£14.99	Jul
Warwickshire (pb)	1-85937-203-1	£9.99	Jul
Worcestershire	1-85937-152-3	£14.99	Jul
Yorkshire Living Memories			
	1-85937-166-3	£14.99	Jul

FRITH PRODUCTS & SERVICES

Francis Frith would doubtless be pleased to know that the pioneering publishing venture he started in 1860 still continues today. More than a hundred and thirty years later, The Francis Frith Collection continues in the same innovative tradition and is now one of the foremost publishers of vintage photographs in the world. Some of the current activities include:

Interior Decoration

Today Frith's photographs can be seen framed and as giant wall murals in thousands of pubs, restaurants, hotels, banks, retail stores and other public buildings throughout the country. In every case they enhance the unique local atmosphere of the places they depict and provide reminders of gentler days in an increasingly busy and frenetic world.

Product Promotions

Frith products have been used by many major companies to promote the sales of their own products or to reinforce their own history and heritage. Brands include Hovis bread, Courage beers, Scots Porage Oats, Colman's mustard, Cadbury's foods, Mellow Birds coffee, Dunhill pipe tobacco, Guinness, and Bulmer's Cider.

Genealogy and Family History

As the interest in family history and roots grows world-wide, more and more people are turning to Frith's photographs of Great Britain for images of the towns, villages and streets where their ancestors lived; and, of course, photographs of the churches and chapels where their ancestors were christened, married and buried are an essential part of every genealogy tree and family album.

A series of easy-to-use CD Roms is planned for publication, and an increasing number of Frith photographs will be able to be viewed on specialist genealogy sites. A growing range of Frith books will be available on CD.

The Internet

Already thousands of Frith photographs can be viewed and purchased on the internet. By the end of the year 2000 some 60,000 Frith photographs will be available on the internet. The number of sites is constantly expanding, each focussing on different products and services from the Collection.

Some of the sites are listed below.

www.townpages.co.uk
www.icollector.com
www.barclaysquare.co.uk
www.cornwall-online.co.uk

For background information on the Collection look at the three following sites:

www.francisfrith.com
www.francisfrith.co.uk
www.frithbook.co.uk

Frith Products

All Frith photographs are available Framed or just as Mounted Prints, and can be ordered from the address below. From time to time other products - Address Books, Calendars, Table Mats, etc - are available.

For further information:
if you would like further information on any of the above aspects of the Frith business please contact us at the address below:
The Francis Frith Collection,
Frith's Barn, Teffont, Salisbury, Wiltshire,
England SP3 5QP.
Tel: +44 (0)1722 716 376 Fax: +44 (0)1722 716 881   Email: uksales@francisfrith.com

---

To receive your FREE Mounted Print

Cut out this Voucher and return it with your remittance for £1.50 to cover postage and handling. Choose any photograph included in this book. Your SEPIA print will be A4 in size, and mounted in a cream mount with burgundy rule lines, overall size 14 x 11 inches.

Order additional Mounted Prints at HALF PRICE (only £7.49 each*)

If there are further pictures you would like to order, possibly as gifts for friends and family, acquire them at half price (no additional postage and handling required).

Have your Mounted Prints framed*

For an additional £14.95 per print you can have your chosen Mounted Print framed in an elegant polished wood and gilt moulding, overall size 16 x 13 inches (no additional postage and handling required).

---

* IMPORTANT!
These special prices are only available if ordered using the original voucher on this page (no copies permitted) and at the same time as your free Mounted Print, for delivery to the same address

---

Voucher for FREE and Reduced Price Frith Prints

Picture no.	Page number	Qty	Mounted @ £7.49	Framed + £14.95	Total Cost
		1	Free of charge*	£	£
			£7.49	£	£
			£7.49	£	£
			£7.49	£	£
			£7.49	£	£
			£7.49	£	£
			* Post & handling		£1.50

Book Title . . . .   **Total Order Cost**   £

Please do not photocopy this voucher. Only the original is valid, so please cut it out and return it to us.

I enclose a cheque / postal order for £ . . . .
made payable to 'The Francis Frith Collection'
OR please debit my Mastercard / Visa / Switch / Amex card

Number . . . .

Expires . . . .   Signature . . . .

Name Mr/Mrs/Ms . . . .

Address . . . .

. . . .

. . . .

. . . . Postcode . . . .

Daytime Tel No . . . .   Valid to 31/12/01

Frith Collectors' Guild

From time to time we publish a magazine of news and stories about Frith photographs and further special offers of Frith products. If you would like 12 months FREE membership, please return this form.

Send completed forms to:
The Francis Frith Collection, Frith's Barn, Teffont, Salisbury, Wiltshire SP3 5QP

The Francis Frith Collectors' Guild

Please enrol me as a member for 12 months free of charge.

Name Mr/Mrs/Ms . . . .

Address . . . .

. . . .

. . . .

. . . . Postcode . . . .

Free Print - see overleaf